WORLD IN VIEW
INDONESIA

Nance Lui Fyson

STECK-VAUGHN
LIBRARY
Austin, Texas

**Published in the United States in 1990 by Steck-Vaughn Co.,
Austin, Texas**, a subsidiary of National Education Corporation.

First published 1989

Published by
Macmillan Children's books
A division of
MACMILLAN PUBLISHERS LTD

Cover: *A Hindu temple on the island of Bali.*
Title page: *Traditional houses in North Sumatra.*

Designed by Julian Holland Publishing Ltd
Picture research by Nance Fyson

Acknowledgments: For Colin

Library of Congress Cataloging-in-Publication Data

Fyson, Nance Lui.
     Indonesia / Nance Lui Fyson.
        p.   cm.—(World in view)
     Includes index.
     Summary: Surveys the people, customs, history,
geography, natural resources, and tourism of Indonesia.
     ISBN 0-8114-2435-9
     1. Indonesia—Juvenile literature. [1. Indonesia.] I. Title.
II. Series.
DS615.F97   1990
915.98—dc20   89-26283
                                                        CIP
                                                        AC

Printed and bound in the United States
1 2 3 4 5 6 7 8 9 0 LB 94 93 92 91 90

Photographic credits: All photographs by Nance Fyson except pgs. 8, 13, 17, 20, 23, 24, 26,
38 and 39 are Robert Harding Picture Library; p. 37 is Ace Photo Agency.

Contents

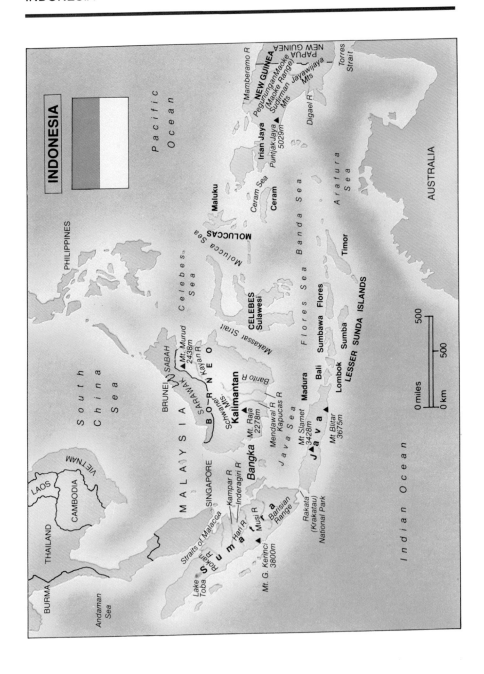

1 Introducing Indonesia

The country of Indonesia is made up of 13,677 tropical islands. Only 3,000 of the islands have people living on them, but Indonesia still manages to have the fifth-largest population in the world. Only China, India, the Soviet Union, and the United States have more people. Over 165 million Indonesians speak hundreds of different languages. It is not surprising that the nation's motto is "Many are one."

A group of many islands is called an "archipelago." Indonesia is the world's largest, stretching out across 3,200 miles of sea.

Fact Box	
Total area	741,098 square miles
Population	147,490,298 (1980 census)
Climate	Jakarta Jan 78°F July 78°F Padang Jan 80°F July 80°F Surabaya Jan 81°F July 78°F
Annual rainfall	Jakarta 71 inches Padang 177 inches Surabaya 51 inches
Highest mountain	Pucak Jaya in Irian Jaya, 16,502 feet

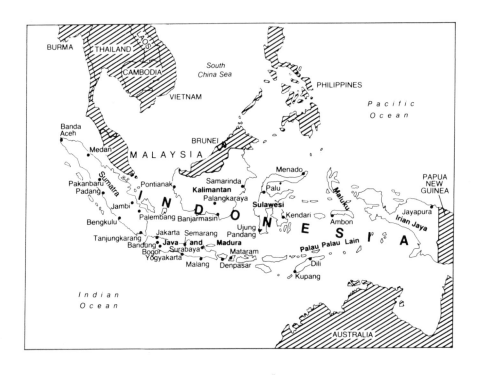

Bahasa Indonesian, a Malayan dialect, is the official language of the Republic of Indonesia, although Dutch is the unofficial language.

The national flag is a horizontal band of red over a band of white and the national anthem is *Indonesia Raya*, sung to a tune written in 1928 by Wage Supratman.

> **The unit of currency** used in Indonesia is the Rupiah, which is divided into 100 Sen. Rupiahs are available in notes of 1, 2.5, 5, 10, 25, 50, 100, 500, 1,000, 5,000, and 10,000 and there are coins of 1, 5, 10, 15, and 50 Sen.

Inner and outer islands

The islands of Java, Bali, Madura, and West Lombok are known as Inner Indonesia, and all the other islands together make up Outer Indonesia. Inner Indonesia has a great many people living closely together and farming, which uses a lot of workers and irrigation. Just one island, Java, supports about two-thirds of the Indonesians on only 7 percent of its land.

Outer Indonesia has thick rain forests and the people there are spread out more. Nearly all of the country's most valuable exports come from the outer islands. Rubber and palm oil are produced in Sumatra. Petroleum, copper, tin, and bauxite come from Sumatra, Bangka, Billiton, and Irian Jaya. Timber comes from Kalimantan.

All the islands of Indonesia are in the most active volcanic region in the world. Four of the huge pieces that make up the Earth's crust are on the move in that area, bumping and grinding together. These moving continental plates cause both earthquakes and volcanic eruptions.

There are hundreds of volcanoes in Indonesia. Over 70 of these are still active and nearly every year a major eruption causes death and destruction. Some volcanoes throw out "acidic" material, and then the land becomes useless for growing crops. However, when volcanoes throw

Timber from Kalimantan is unloaded in the old harbor at Jakarta, Java.

out "basic" material as on Java, Bali, and a few other islands, the soil becomes much more fertile. Java and Bali now have the most fertile tropical soils in the world for this reason. More rice is grown on each acre of rice field than anywhere else in the world.

Climate

As well as being volcanic, all the islands are also tropical. Temperatures at sea level are much the same from place to place and change only a few degrees throughout the year, ranging from 78°F to 82°F. In the mountains it is usually slightly cooler.

Krakatoa

One of the largest volcanic explosions in the world happened in Indonesia. In 1883 the volcano of Krakatoa blew up. The noise of the explosion was heard 3,000 miles away. This huge explosion caused a massive tidal wave that killed about 36,000 people and made an ash cloud that affected the world's weather for several years. A smaller volcano appeared in the same spot. It is called Anah Krakatoa which means son of Krakatoa.

Mount Batur is an active volcano on Bali that last erupted in 1963. Eruptions cause loss of life but help soil fertility.

Most of the islands are within the equatorial "everwet" zone, with at least three inches of rain falling every month. Most islands have much more rain than this during the time of the northeast monsoon, November to April. (A monsoon is a high wind that usually brings rain.) A few places, like Bogor in West Java, have rain almost daily throughout the year. The southeast monsoon blows hot, dry air between May and October on most islands.

Wildlife

While the climate is similar across the islands, plant life is immensely varied, with about 40,000 different species. The variety of animal life is unlike anywhere else in the world. There are over 500 mammals and over 1,500 species of birds. In line with worldwide concern for conservation, more than 6 percent of Indonesia's land area is protected. There is a system of National Parks, Nature Reserves, and Protected Forests.

The very first National Park in Indonesia was Ujong Kulon, on the southwestern tip of Java. The park has such animals as wild pigs, leaf monkeys, green turtles, and many birds. The most famous animal at Ujong Kulon is the now rare one-horned Java rhinoceros. There is a small herd of about 60 rhinos in the park and these are the last of their kind anywhere.

Another protected animal now found only in one part of Indonesia is the monitor lizard. The largest of these are also called Komodo Dragons because they live on Komodo, a hilly island that is part of Nusa Tenggara. These "dragons" are not really dragons, of course, but simply very large lizards. Small monitor lizards eat insects, while larger ones feed on birds and frogs. Komodo Dragons are so big that they can kill and eat deer and wild pigs, as well as goats.

Visitors to Komodo are taken "dragon spotting" in the months from May to September. Guides lead the way to a feeding spot where the hissing "dragons" come to eat dead goats.

Java and Bali

Far away from dragons are two of the main islands in Indonesia called Java and Bali. Java is the hub of Indonesia and has the nation's capital city of Jakarta. About 70 percent of the people work in farming, and fishing is also an important occupation. People living on the island of Bali are

Water buffalo are used to pull this farmer's plow in Bali. The flooded field will be used to plant rice.

11

mostly farmers as well. Tourism is another source of jobs as the southern tip of Bali is a resort area, with luxury hotels and beaches.

Farmers in Java and Bali use *sawah* agriculture, which means growing rice in flooded paddy fields. This needs rich soil and plenty of water but does produce a lot of food. The farmers help each other to irrigate the land and to harvest. The sawah communities of Java and Bali are quite different from communities on the outer islands.

Sumatra

Sumatra is third biggest of the Indonesian islands in area and is second in population, with over 30 million people. The island is first in importance for exports which include oil, natural gas, rubber, tin, tea, coffee, palm oil, timber, and tobacco.

Of Sumatra's 90 volcanoes, 15 are still active. They release acidic material that prevents the soil from being fertile. To make the soil richer, many farmers still use a method called swidden or "slash-and-burn." Farmers clear and burn the forest just before the heavy rains fall. This helps to fertilize the land but forests are being lost at an alarming rate. More and more farmers are now using irrigation and chemical fertilizers instead.

Nusa Tenggara

Farmers also use slash-and-burn methods on the islands of Nusa Tenggara. These are mostly dry islands and the raising of livestock is important. People export cattle and horses to pay for goods imported from Java. There are few minerals and the islands are much less developed than other parts of the archipelago.

A village on the river in Kalimantan, the southern two-thirds of the island of Borneo.

Riau

By contrast, the province of Riau with over 3,000 islands is full of natural resources. Riau is one of the richest parts of Indonesia, with oil and tin as the main exports. The mainland is covered in thick jungle and swamps, but other islands in the province are more varied.

Kalimantan

Kalimantan, the southern two-thirds of the island of Borneo, also has mineral resources. The northern part of Borneo includes the states of Sarawak and Sabah, which are part of Malaysia.

Kalimantan people are mainly farmers but there are also large reserves of oil, natural gas, and even diamonds. Matapura is the diamond capital, where over 30,000 people are employed in the diamond mines. There are also hundreds of people working in factories to polish the gems.

Irian Jaya

Irian Jaya is also just part of an island, New Guinea, which is the second largest island in the world. The western half became part of Indonesia in 1963, and the eastern half has been an independent nation called Papua New Guinea since 1975. Irian Jaya, the Indonesian part, is one of the most isolated areas on Earth today. There are dense jungles, mountains, and few roads.

Maluku

While Irian Jaya is quite large, the thousand islands of Maluku Province are fairly small. Some of these were the Spice Islands that attracted Indian, Chinese, Arab, and European traders centuries ago. Trees producing the spices nutmeg, mace, and cloves still grow there.

The Spice Islands, or "Moluccas," are important in Indonesia's history, because spices and other resources prompted Europeans to take over the islands as a colony. It is only since World War II that the country has become an independent nation.

2   Colony to Free Nation

Some of the first people who ever lived made their home in what is now Indonesia. Long before the birth of Christ, there were people on the islands growing rice and working with metals like copper, bronze, and iron. These people were also good sailors, traveling great distances. From about the first century A.D. there were close contacts between people on the islands and India. Different empires rose and fell. For example, the Srivijaya empire based on Sumatra lasted from about the seventh to thirteenth centuries.

The Venetian Marco Polo was the first European to visit the archipelago, in 1292. Portuguese and Spanish explorers followed, and then the English and Dutch. By the late 1600s, the Dutch East India Company controlled most of Java as well as ports on other islands. The archipelago was then known as the Dutch East Indies or the Netherland Indies.

In the early 1800s, the British took over the Dutch East Indies for several years, but by 1816 it was back under Dutch control. Dutch interest centered on producing export crops such as sugar and coffee, and crops that would feed local people were neglected. This meant serious food shortages.

Move for independence
By the early 1900s most of the Indonesia of today was under Dutch rule, and islanders were starting to ask for independence. In 1908 some medical students in Java began a society that

Dried flower buds from this tree are used to make cloves, a highly valued spice. Profits from spices, plantation crops like coffee, and minerals like oil, made the Dutch want to keep Indonesia as a colony.

became political a few years later. Other students formed study clubs. One of these was headed by a young man named Sukarno, who began the Indonesian Nationalist Party (PNI) in 1927 to press for freedom from Dutch rule.

The Dutch wanted to keep the islands as a colony and so tried to stop the nationalist groups. Leaders like Sukarno were sent to outer islands and were not allowed to come back until the Japanese invaded during World War II. The Japanese not only freed leaders but also put hundreds of Indonesians in government jobs. This all helped to encourage the independence movement.

On August 17, 1945, Sukarno proclaimed Indonesia an independent nation. However, it was not until December 27, 1949, that the

16

Republic of the United States of Indonesia came into being, with a new constitution. The new republic began on August 17, 1950, with the city of Jakarta as its capital. Later that year Indonesia became a member of the United Nations.

Sukarno, who led the Indonesian Revolution, is regarded as the father of his country. His own father followed the Islamic religion while his mother was a Hindu. Sukarno believed that the different religions and types of people on the islands could be united into one nation. He said: " . . . the color of our skins may differ, the shape of our noses and foreheads may differ: Irians are black, Sumatrans brown, Javanese are short, people of the Moluccas taller . . . but no more are we islanders and strangers. Today we are Indonesians and we are one . . ."

People on Biak Island, just one of the many ethnic groups united to make a nation state.

By the early 1960s, Indonesia seemed to be moving toward Communism. The Indonesian Communist Party was the first such party in Southeast Asia. By 1965, the Party had about three million members and another 17 million followers, making it the largest Communist party in the non-Communist world.

The Communist Party tried to take over the Indonesian government in 1965. Although this coup failed, Sukarno seemed in sympathy with the Communists. He refused to speak against them and did nothing to stop the party from trying to take power. Thousands were killed in the years 1965–66 and this is remembered as a dark time in the country's history.

Suharto takes over

Another leader, General Suharto, *did* act against the Communists, which won him support from the Indonesian people. In 1966, Suharto and other military leaders managed to ban the Communist Party. In 1968, the People's Consultative Assembly formally elected Suharto as president for the next five years. Sukarno was no longer popular and died in 1970.

With Suharto as leader, Indonesia cooperated more with other nations. The Republic also made more efforts to attract investment from abroad. Most foreign investment in Indonesia now comes from Japan, which is also Indonesia's biggest trading partner. Suharto has continued as president into the 1980s. The president's term of office is five years, and Suharto is elected and reelected by a People's Consultative Congress (MPR).

President Suharto's government follows the *Pancasila* (Five Principles) in governing the country. The Indonesian coat of arms has symbols showing these five points:

1. **Faith in God** A star stands for the idea that all Indonesians should believe in a god.
2. **Humanity** The chain shows that people worldwide are united and that Indonesia is part of that chain.
3. **Nationalism** A buffalo heads stands for the united country. All groups of people in Indonesia must join together as one nation.
4. **Representative government** The banyan tree stands for village democracy. Representatives meet and try to reach a decision on which they all agree.
5. **Social Justice** Rice and cotton are symbols of a fair society that will give food and clothing for all.

Jakarta

Nationally, Indonesia is governed from the city of Jakarta where over seven million people live. There are a few skyscrapers in the city center, but the rest of the buildings are mostly small, with only one or two stories.

Jakarta is on a site that was once a major port for exporting pepper during the fifteenth and sixteenth centuries. It was called Jayakarta at that time, then Batavia. The Dutch East India Company controlled Batavia during the seventeenth century and the town grew rich on trade in pepper, cloves, nutmeg, tea, textiles, sugar, hardwoods, and rice. Batavia was then just a small walled town built to look very much like Amsterdam.

19

The city of Jakarta, capital of Indonesia. There are a few tall buildings and highways, but most of Jakarta consists of low buildings and narrow streets.

In the eighteenth century there were hard times and epidemics of diseases like malaria and cholera. Then, in the nineteenth century, Batavia began to thrive again. It was not until the 1940s that it was renamed Jakarta and became a city. After independence the city grew quickly as more Indonesians arrived from the countryside and the outer islands.

Some of Jakarta's history can still be seen today. For example, the port of Sunda Kelapa has traditional wooden *pinisi* sailing boats. Each day 70 to 80 of these boats come in from Kalimantan with sawn timber. The area around the port is rich in history as well. Across the river is a nineteenth-century Dutch lookout tower. Behind it is a structure built in 1652 by the Dutch to store tea, coffee, and Indian cloth. This is now a museum with sailing craft from all over Indonesia.

Three other buildings from Dutch colonial times have also been made into museums. The Jakarta History Museum shows mainly furnishings and portraits, the Wayang Museum displays many puppets and masks, and the Fine Arts Museum exhibits paintings and sculpture by modern Indonesian artists.

Although Jakarta is now the center of government and there are a number of other cities, over 90 percent of Indonesian people live in the country's 66,000 villages. Who *are* all these varied people who now comprise the Republic of Indonesia?

3 People, People, People

The people of Indonesia are now united as one nation, but there are over 100 different ethnic groups. Each group has its own culture, style of housing and dress, and its own language. The people vary in looks as well—from color of skin, to hair, body size, and the way faces are shaped.

The first people to arrive on the islands thousands of years ago were dark skinned and very small. Another wave of people came a few centuries later and they were also dark skinned with broad, flat noses. Then, after many centuries came a third wave of people. They were much more like the Chinese, with lighter skin and almond-shaped eyes. Another wave of people followed, also looking much like the Chinese. A number of these people have mixed together, creating still more varieties, but other people have stayed as quite separate groups.

Some general statements may be made about people and cultures in Indonesia. For example, it is not considered polite to stand with hands on hips while talking, because this is thought to be an angry gesture.

Indonesians are generally very courteous people and try very hard not to offend. For the *Javanese* especially, *Ru kun,* meaning harmony, is the goal. Being well mannered and reserved is very important to them. While these ideas are common throughout Indonesia, there are also many local differences among ethnic groups.

Men of the Dani tribe in West Irian. Their features are like those of Australian Aboriginals. The wooden farming tool being carried is used for digging the earth.

Differences

Here is an example of one difference: In West Sumatra the *Minangkabau* people are "matriarchal." This means that women head the families, and property is passed on from mother to daughter. The *Batak* people of North Sumatra are a "patriarchal" group. Men control the society and pass property to their sons.

Another difference is that most people in Irian Jaya are described as *Papuan* because they are similar to the people of neighboring Papua New Guinea. Irian Jaya people have dark skin, woolly hair, broad, flat noses, and they look very much like the Aborigines of Australia. This is quite different from the lighter skins and Malay features of most Indonesians.

23

A Toradjanese musician from Sulawesi has oriental facial features. She plays a flute made from a length of bamboo.

Some groups are larger in number than others. For example, North Sumatra has more *Achenese* people than any other single group. The Achenese are nearly all farmers but they are also good at metalwork, weaving, pottery, and boat-building. The *Badui* people live in West Java and are hunters as well as farmers. *Bugis* are from around southern Sulawesi and have colorful wind-driven boats. *Dayak* people live along the rivers in Borneo. They are skilled in many arts, such as woodcarving, metalworking, weaving, mat and basket making. The *Minahasa* are farming people in northern Sulawesi. *Sundanese* live in the highlands of West Java. The *Toradjanese* people in central Sulawesi are hunters and makers of bark cloth. Javanese people, most of

Wayan is the first child in his family and has a Balinese "number name." He is 18 years old and earns his school tuition by selling rings to tourists on a beach. Wayan studies subjects like math, geography, and history and there is even a subject called "tourism."

Names

Sometimes names show the group to which people belong. For example, Javanese often have only one name, and that is likely to be a family name. Common family names end in "o," such as Suharto or Widodo. Minangkabau personal names often sound Islamic, with the letter "z," such as Rizal and Faizal.

Names in Indonesia can also show a person's status and social level, and may even show what work the family does. In Bali, where Hindu people are split into higher, middle, and lower groups called castes, there is a system for naming children according to the order of their birth. The highest caste or group of people, the Brahmana, name the first child Putu, the second child Made, the third Nyoman, and the fourth child Ketut. If a fifth child is born, they start again with the name Putu. The middle caste doesn't use number naming but the lowest caste does—starting Wayan, then Made, Nyoman, and Ketut. So if someone is called Wayan, he or she is either the first or fifth child in a family.

whom live on the island of Java, call themselves *Jawa*. Yet another large group of people in Indonesia are the Overseas Chinese who came, or whose ancestors came, over the last hundred years. The Chinese now live mainly in port cities.

Housing

Houses are more than just homes in Indonesia. Each ethnic group of people has its own style of building which is both symbolic and important to the culture of that group. However, in some parts of the country, traditional homes are no longer

This Toraja house in Sulawesi follows traditional style. Nearby rice barns look similar but are much smaller.

being built. Modern Javanese houses made of brick and cement with galvanized iron roofs are being seen more throughout the islands.

The Toradja people of Sulawesi have a traditional house with a long roof that rises up at both ends. Their houses all face to the north, which is where they believe their gods live. The wall panels are decorated with paintings of buffalo, and a carving of a buffalo's head is put on the front of the house. Older homes have roofs of overlapping bamboo but newer houses use corrugated metal sheets. Inside are just two or three rooms with small windows and doors.

When a traditional house is to be built, a chicken, pig, or buffalo is killed as a sacrifice beforehand. Then, when the house is finished, people celebrate with a large feast of pork and buffalo meat, followed by dancing.

Toradja houses face a row of rice barns, which are also decorated. The area for storing rice is just under seven feet off the ground. The storage area stands on four pillars that are polished smooth so that rats cannot climb up and eat the rice.

The Batak people living in Sumatra build houses on stilts, one or two yards off the ground. Their house walls are made of wood, with a roof of either sugar palm fiber or modern, but less attractive, corrugated iron. The roof bends upward at each end, where it rises to a sharp

In a Balinese compound, each family has its own open veranda for sitting, as well as a few closed rooms.

27

point. Decorations include buffalo horns as well as carvings of lizards and monster heads.

With these houses, the space below is used for animals like cows, pigs, and goats. The living space of the house itself is large, with no dividing wall. Rattan mats are lowered at night to give some privacy around small sections. As many as a dozen families may live together in such a house.

The Dayak people of Kalimantan have traditional "longhouses," which are just that—long houses. A village may be several smaller longhouses or just one large one. The homes are built on wooden piles as much as 10 feet high. This protects families from dangers such as flooding and wild animals, and logs are used as stairs up to the house. Animals such as pigs and chickens are kept below the house. Each longhouse is split into separate sections for each family, but there is also a long porch running the length of the building that is used by everyone. There rice is pounded and meetings are held.

Traditional houses in Bali are different again. A wider family including cousins, aunts, and grandparents may live together inside a compound. This has a high wall surrounding a number of separate buildings. Each couple and their children have a building to themselves, often with a large covered porch or veranda for sitting. There is a building that is shared for cooking, and a building for washing. There is also a family temple.

The family compound is entered through an entrance backed with a small wall *aling aling*. This is to stop evil spirits from entering, as such spirits are believed to find it difficult to turn corners.

Mutual help

One important tradition in Indonesia is called *Gotong Royong* which means "mutual help." People help one another with work, such as planting and harvesting rice, building houses, and making irrigation canals. People help each other with play and celebrations as well.

Mutual help is displayed more formally by the whole cooperative movement. People join together in a cooperative to work at growing crops, rearing farm animals, fishing, and also making handicrafts for sale. Millions of people now belong to over 25,000 cooperatives and the numbers are growing.

Arisan is another kind of mutual help. The members of an arisan group, usually women, meet once a month for a special meal. They each

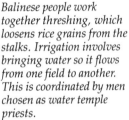

Balinese people work together threshing, which loosens rice grains from the stalks. Irrigation involves bringing water so it flows from one field to another. This is coordinated by men chosen as water temple priests.

put a set amount of money into a pot, then a name is drawn to be that month's winner of all the money. The arisan exists until every person has had the chance to win. These groups also buy appliances such as sewing machines for the members, since buying in bulk means a cheaper price for each person.

Most Indonesians generally like to be with others rather than by themselves. They do not expect the sort of privacy that many people from North America or Europe think is necessary.

The many ethnic groups share what is sometimes called *jam karet* or "rubber time." When someone says they will arrive or call, it is not likely to be at a specific hour on the clock. Time is often much looser. The 24-hour day is roughly divided into *pagi* (midnight to 11 a.m.), *siang* (11 a.m. to 3 p.m.), *sore* (3 p.m. to 6:45 p.m.) and *malam* (6:45 p.m. to midnight). Someone is more likely to say they will arrive siang than to say they will arrive at 12:30 p.m.

In a similar way, someone from North America or Europe might plan a dinner party with a set number of guests for a particular time. However, Indonesians would be more likely to entertain by having a large number of people at a buffet meal to celebrate a family event. People would come and go and there would not be a definite number of guests.

Special occasions
Meals with many guests help to celebrate main changes in life. Weddings are so important that families may go into debt and even sell land and livestock to pay for a reception. In Bali there are

two main kinds of marriage. The family of the man may visit the family of the woman to formally propose marriage. Elopement is the other choice. The couple go into hiding, and when they come out the marriage is official.

Wedding clothes vary somewhat from place to place. For example, the traditional bride on Java would wear a fitted, black velvet jacket and a wrapped skirt made of fine *batik* cloth. A Sundanese bride would wear a white blouse instead of the black jacket. Minangkabau brides wear ornate gold headdresses and red or bright blue costumes.

The birth of a child is also an important time. Women are given a special bathing while they are pregnant. In Bali this is at the third month of pregnancy but it is usually at seven months elsewhere in the Republic.

After a child is born there is a ceremony to welcome the child to the world. This is common throughout Indonesia, with some variations from place to place. When a Batak child is seven days old, the mother pounds rice cakes with sugar and spices and offers them to villagers as she shows the baby the sun for the first time. In Bali, a baby's feet are not allowed to touch the ground until a special ceremony takes place 210 days after birth. The child is then officially welcomed and its hair is cut.

Birth control

Every year over three million babies are added to Indonesia's population. Families are still larger, on average, than in North America or Europe. However, since 1967 the Indonesian government

This large family-planning poster in a village reminds people that the ideal family has no more than two children.

has been encouraging people to have fewer children. There is a National Family Planning Board that has been very successful in lowering the birth rate. *Dua Anak Cukup*, meaning "two children are enough" is the popular slogan. Even the five-rupiah coin shows a mother, father, and two children.

Posters, billboards, radio, and television all encourage people to use family planning. One poster shows a motorbike with a man, woman, and two children. The message is that you can fit the whole family on a motorbike if you only have two children! There are thousands of field workers that go from door to door delivering contraceptives. In some places houses are coded with little symbols near the front door. These show what kind of birth control device each family is using.

People may be given rewards for using birth control. A woman who agrees to use contraceptives is called "*apsari*," the Indonesian word for "angel." New angels are sometimes given gifts, such as a load of rice.

Birth control is needed because more and more people being born puts pressure on a country's resources. If Indonesia keeps growing the way it is growing now, the population is likely to double in size by the year 2035. How could the country provide enough extra food, homes, jobs, schools, and health care for so many people?

Transmigration

The main population problem is on Java, and also on Bali. On Java there are about 1,900 people per square mile. This is more than *twice* the density of New Jersey, which is the most densely populated state in the United States.

While Java is very crowded, other islands in Indonesia are only sparsely populated. Sumatra has only about 179 people per square mile, Sulawesi has about 158 per square mile, Kalimantan has about 36 per square mile, and Irian Jaya has only about 15 people per square mile.

Besides encouraging couples to have fewer children, the government has also been trying to move people to less-populated islands. These transmigration programs started as early as 1905 when the Dutch tried moving people from Java. In the early 1970s, the Suharto government moved 182,000 people out of Java, Bali, and Lombok. The aim was to move over a million people in the mid-1970s, but only half this was achieved. The government tried to move over a million people in the late 1970s and early 1980s.

Every family that moves in this way is given an area of land for building a house and land for growing crops. In the beginning, families are supplied with food and seedlings, farm tools, kitchen utensils, and carpenter's tools. People are also given guidance on how best to grow crops on the local soil.

Languages

With so many ethnic groups, there are also over 350 distinct languages and dialects. However, there is also a national language called Bahasa Indonesia, which people speak in addition to their own local language.

In some ways, Indonesian is a fairly simple language to learn. There are no words like "the"

Here are a few Indonesian words and phrases:

Good morning	selamat pagi
Good night	selamat malam
Thank you	terima kasih
Please	silakan

or "a." To say a room is dirty in Indonesian is *kamar kotor*, "room dirty." Sometimes a plural is made by simply doubling the word. "Child" is *anak* and "children" is *anak anak*. However, there are some complications. For example, Javanese, Balinese, and Sundanese languages have different words that are used when speaking to a "lower" person, "higher" person, or an "equal."

When speaking to an older man, an Indonesian would call him *bapak* (father) or simply *pak*. In the same way, an Indonesian would call an older woman *ibu* (mother) or simply *bu*.

Children in Indonesia learn at an early age to honor older people and fathers especially. Calling an older man bapak is to honor him. Indonesians are taught to respect those with higher status and to avoid *malu*, embarrassment. Families should not be let down.

4 Beliefs and Celebrations

Islam is the most popular religion on nearly all of the crowded inner and less-crowded outer islands. Over 85 percent of Indonesian people are Muslim. Christianity, Hinduism, and Buddhism are the other main religions followed.

Islam

An Arab prophet named Mohammed, born about 570 A.D., founded the Islamic religion to spread the Word of God. People who follow Mohammed's teachings and the Islamic religion are called Muslims. They believe that peace comes by surrendering to this one God, Allah. The word *Islam* comes from a word *Salam* which means "peace" as well as "surrender."

The holy book of the Muslims is called the Koran, and much of it tells Muslims how they should behave. Pork is not eaten by strict Muslims and alcoholic drink is not allowed.

Arab settlers brought their religion to Indonesia in the seventh century A.D. Muslims in Indonesia now practice their religion in a somewhat different way from Muslims in Arab countries. For example, women in Indonesia do not have to wear veils to cover their faces, and they have more freedom. Another difference is that Muslim men in Indonesia may have only two wives—and then only if the first wife agrees. Elsewhere, Muslim men may have as many as four wives.

A mosque on the Maluku Islands. In front of the main building are two minarets. Inside the mosque, the faithful kneel on the floor to pray.

Ramadan, the most important Islamic festival, happens in the ninth month of the Muslim calendar. For one month, people get up early to eat and then go without food (fast) the whole day, from sunrise until sunset. During this month, many Muslims visit family graves to say prayers and to sprinkle the graves with holy water. At the

37

end of Ramadan there is *Lebaran (Idul Fitri)*, which is a two-day public holiday. There are processions, and people exchange gifts. People also ask to be forgiven for anything they have done wrong. During Ramadan, Muslims say prayers at home and also in religious buildings called mosques. Prayers are said at mosques during the rest of the year as well, principally on Friday afternoons. Government offices and many businesses close to allow time for prayers.

Mosques often have a high dome over a prayer hall. One wall inside has a niche to show the direction of Mecca. Muslims regard the city of Mecca in Saudi Arabia as their holy place and face toward it when they pray. In the mosque there is also a raised pulpit and a stand to hold the Koran. A fountain, pool, or water jug provides water for holy ceremonies. There are no seats or decorations inside a mosque.

Outside the mosque building is a towerlike minaret where a person known as a *muezzin* used to call people to prayer. However, modern technology has even touched religion. A cassette recording is now used in many places.

Most office and commercial buildings have a *musholla*, which is a place for prayer. Even airports set aside a room, marked with a sign. Muslims are expected to say prayers five times a day and to wash each time before praying.

Other festivals
Besides national festivals like Ramadan, some islands have their own particular celebrations. For example, in the Riau islands there is a Festival of the Sea, held in the second month of the Islamic

calendar. People hang packs of sticky rice on trees near the beach. Logs are cut from the forest and taken by canoe to deep water and dropped in. This is meant to please the spirits of the ocean so they will keep people from drowning.

In the town of Pariaman in West Sumatra, a colorful Islamic festival called *Tabut* is held each year in honor of Mohammed's grandchildren, who were killed defending their faith. A winged, horselike creature called a *bouraq* is part of the festival. Villages nearby make bouraqs and paint them in bright colors. Gold necklaces and other decorations are put on the creatures. The bouraqs are carried through the streets with much fun and dancing and then thrown into the sea. People dive in afterward and try to grab the gold necklaces and other souvenirs. Visitors now come from all over Indonesia to enjoy the festivities.

Bali Hinduism
The island of Bali is different from most of Indonesia in that most Balinese people are Hindu, not Muslim. However, Hinduism on Bali is not quite like Hinduism in India. The people of Bali worship Brahma, Shiva, and Vishnu, but do not make statues or pictures of the gods.

A Balinese temple usually has a series of courtyards. Worshipers need not be barefoot, but they have to wear temple scarves as sashes around their waists. Cockfights are a part of temple ceremonies and men keep fighting cocks as prize pets. They can sometimes be seen in bell-shaped cane baskets outside homes. Women take offerings of fruit and flowers to the temple, carried in huge pyramids on their heads. The

Women go to a Balinese Hindu temple, each woman balancing on her head an offering of fruit. The women wear traditional sarongs, cloth tied as long skirts.

women balance their amazing and colorful loads beautifully as they walk.

Village temples are arranged so that the holiest shrines face toward mountains. The Balinese believe that mountains are holy, while the sea is the source of evil. Balinese don't like living beside the sea, which is unusual for an island people. This is why the old capital of Bali in the eleventh century A.D. was in the center of the island. The

Balinese make processions to the sea but this is to make offerings so that evil spirits will not harm their villages.

The Hindu New Year on Bali is called *Nyepi*. This happens during the month of March and marks the end of the rainy season. On the day before, villages are cleaned and much cooking is done. Then on the evening before, there are parades in which people carry large papier maché

This ten-foot-high papier maché demon was made for the Balinese New Year. It will be carried through the streets on New Year's Eve, to chase evil from the village.

figures that look like demons. A great deal of noise is made to chase away evil spirits. On New Year's Day, everyone is supposed to stay at home and relax. The roads are empty because no one is supposed to travel.

Life forces
Belief in good and evil spirits is a common part of religion in Indonesia. "Animism" also plays an important part. This is the belief that there are "life forces" in plants, animals, and objects like rocks and trees—and even in whole villages and nations. This special life force is called *semangat*.

Indonesians believe that semangat in people is strongest in the head, and especially in the hair. Long ago there were some tribes who went headhunting. They would kill someone and bring back the head to hang up. This was thought to keep sickness and bad luck away.

Indonesians (and many other Asians) do not like being touched on the head because it is felt to be sacred. In Javanese culture a "lower" person should not have his or her head above a "higher" person. A Javanese may lower his or her head and drop his or her shoulders to show respect.

People's hair is supposed to have a lot of semangat, and a ceremony is held when a child has his or her first haircut. There is also an exchange of hair clippings as part of the marriage ceremony. People who follow traditional beliefs are careful to make sure that their hair clippings cannot fall into the hands of an enemy witch!

Blood is also thought to have semangat. In parts of Indonesia, new house pillars have animal blood put on them to make the house strong.

A Balinese temple to the goddess of rice, Dewi Sri, is out in the middle of a rice field. Offerings are made asking for a good harvest.

There is semangat in plants as well. For example, Dewi Sri is the goddess of the sacred rice spirit. When the rice is being harvested, people treat the grains with great respect. They may even apologize as they cut the rice plants. Other important plants such as coffee are also thought to have a soul.

Food plants and food in general all have a part to play in religious beliefs. Foods are offered to spirits, blessed, and then eaten by the group. One example in Java is the *selamatan*, which means a "safe-guarding." Special foods are eaten, usually yellow rice spiced with tumeric and meat dishes. Incense is burned and prayers are said. A selamatan is usually given for occasions like a birth, a death, or a new building, but it may be given for other reasons as well.

5 Roast Dragonflies!

In Bali, people hungry for a snack may catch dragonflies on sticky sticks and roast the flies. Eels with chili sauce are popular in West Sumatra. In Sulawesi, fried forest rat, stewed bat, and spicy dog meat are eaten. Leg of goat soup is another favorite with some Indonesians. Visitors from North America or Europe might not like these foods, but there are many Indonesian dishes visitors would find more familiar and very tasty indeed.

Rice and noodles

Rice is a main food for both feasts and everyday meals. The most common food for an Indonesian is *nasi goreng*. This simply means fried (goreng) rice (nasi). The rice may have only a few bits of vegetables in it or it may also have onion, red peppers, soy sauce, and even some meat. Last night's leftover rice might be served in the morning as nasi goreng with a fried egg on top.

Another possibility for breakfast is *bubur*, rice . porridge. If you were offered *telur mata sapi, nasi putih*, and *kerupuk*, this would be fried egg, white rice, and a shrimp cracker.

Some foods like nasi goreng are general to Indonesia as a whole. There are also particular dishes and styles of cooking linked to specific areas. Solo in Central Java is well known for its *nasi liwet* (white rice and chicken in coconut cream) and *nasi padang* from West Sumatra uses rice with a whole variety of side dishes. Padang cooking is known for being especially hot and

Lunch in a cafe is mainly a bowl of noodles with small, spicy side dishes.

spicy! The Dutch word *rijstaffel*, "rice table," is used to describe a meal of many single dishes served with rice. There are even sweet cakes made with rice, often with coconut or banana.

Sometimes rice is cooked in small containers made of banana leaves and then eaten cold. Shops sell little bundles of food called *bungkusan* which are usually rice and condiments in banana leaves, skewered closed with a small sharp stick. The leaf is a dish for cooking, a container for carrying-out food, and then a plate to eat off when the bundle is open!

Noodles are also popular in Indonesia. *Bakmi goreng* (fried noodles) may have bits of vegetables, meat, and spices mixed in. There is even *mee kuah*—noodle soup.

45

Cassava

Another filling food eaten mainly by poorer people in Indonesia is called *ubi kayu* or cassava. These are large roots grown below the ground. Once the roots are dug up, cassava does not keep well so everyone has to lend a hand to process the plants quickly. Groups of children help to peel the tubers which are then sliced and dried in the sun. There is a poison in raw cassava roots so they must be boiled very well to make them safe to eat. The slices can be pounded or ground to make tapioca flour. Bags of tapioca flour and also rice flours are sold in shops and supermarkets. About 10 percent of all the calories eaten in Indonesia come from roots and tubers like cassava.

Maluku and other parts of Eastern Indonesia rely on sago, which comes from a palm tree, as

The starchy roots in the center are cassava, also called tapioca or "ubi."

This traditional cooking stove is shared by several related families in a Balinese village compound. Firewood and the dried husks of coconuts are used for fuel. There is also a small paraffin (kerosene) stove in the room set aside as a kitchen. Bottled gas is used for cooking in the cities, and a few well-off city dwellers have microwave ovens.

their main staple food. The tree is cut down and the starch inside is scooped out. A whole family can live for months from the starch of just one tree trunk. Sago bread is made in Maluku and looks like thick wafers. Another use for sago is *papeda*, which involves straining the pulp from the sago palm and boiling it to make a hot porridgelike dish. Sago is also mixed with brown sugar to make a kind of fudge.

Meat

Rice and noodles are often eaten with some kind of meat, and lamb is the favorite in most parts of Indonesia. Beef from cows is eaten in Java but buffalo meat is more common in Sumatra. Buffalo meat is tough and needs to be cooked for a long time, but once cooked it will keep in an airtight jar for up to a month. People in Indonesia who follow the Islamic religion strictly do not eat pork. However, on Bali many people are Hindu, and they do like to eat pork.

Indonesians like to eat using a spoon or fork or just the fingers of the right hand. Since all Indonesian meat dishes use meat sliced small and thin, a knife is not necessary. Meat is not served in a large piece as in America or Europe.

Duck is popular for feasts, and duck eggs are used more than hen eggs in cooking. Many families keep a flock of ducks. These are led out to the flooded rice paddy each day by a duck shepherd holding a stick with a small flag tied to the top. At the rice paddy, the stick is put in the ground and when sunset comes the ducks gather around the stick waiting to be led home again. In the early evening, flocks of ducks can be seen making their way home, led by their shepherds.

Coconuts
There are coconut trees all over Indonesia and the nuts are used frequently in cooking. They may be used both when they are young and when they are fairly old. *Santen* (coconut milk) is a mixture of water and the oils that can be pressed from grated coconut flesh. Santen is used in Indonesian cooking to thicken sauces and add flavor. Any dried-up gratings left at the end are fed to the family hens.

Gudeg is a favorite dish in central Java. It is made of chicken, thick santen, a jackfruit, and spices including chili powder, garlic, cumin, and coriander. Coconut is even used for another Javanese favorite, fried chicken. The Javanese boil the chicken first in rich spices and coconut cream for several hours and then deep fry for about a minute to crisp the outer coating.

Coconut flesh and santen are used in many other Indonesian recipes as well, including cakes and puddings. *Ondé-ondé* are small rice cakes rolled in grated coconut. *Dadar gulung* is a pancake with a coconut filling.

Fruits

The jackfruit, cooked with coconut milk and chicken, is only one of many fruits grown on the islands. Some tropical fruits like bananas, pineapples, mangoes, and papayas are quite familiar to people living in North America or Europe. Watermelons are plentiful on Java and sold cheaply at roadside stands. However, other

A fruit seller. The fruit in the bottom right corner is mangosteen.

The durian is a large, green fruit with a hard, spiky covering. Although the inside is quite tasty, many people find the smell very unpleasant!

fruits that are very common in Indonesia would be quite a novelty to people who had never been to that part of the world.

Salak is known as the snakeskin fruit because of its rough, scaly shell. The fruit inside tastes almost like an apple. The *rambutan* is a bright red fruit covered in hairy spines (*rambut* means "hair" in Indonesian). The white, juicy flesh inside a rambutan tastes a little like a lychee.

Mangosteen has a thick purple skin with segments of white flesh inside. This delicious fruit is often included in offerings to the gods. *Jambu* is a smaller fruit and it grows on tall trees. Passion fruits can be either bright orange or dark purple and make a delicious fruit drink.

Fruit drinks like apple, orange, and mango juice may be sold in cartons. There is even a carton drink made from green beans. Street vendors put crushed ice and one of a variety of fruit concentrates together in a small plastic bag. Little children can be seen on the street happily holding their bag and sipping the liquid through a straw. Roadside stands also have coconuts that are cut in half. The milk inside is refreshing and good to drink.

Soft drinks such as cola are also for sale. Beer is fairly expensive in Indonesia and the wine is usually rice wine. Both coffee and tea are grown on the islands, and may be served quite strong.

Seafood
Just as local tropical fruits are used, so the waters around the islands supply a wide variety of seafood. Turtle soup, grilled turtle, and barbecued squid are all favorites, and so is lobster. Carp is just one of many types of fish that are caught. *Terasi* is a dark-colored paste made from shrimp and nearly all Javanese dishes use at least a little of this. Very small, dried shrimp can be bought either raw or cooked.

Eating out
People may carry an entire meal in a series of stacked containers held together by a long handle called a *rantang*. Office workers in cities often have their lunch delivered this way.

There are many street vendors with snacks and foods of various kinds. They are known as *kaki lima* men and they push their wheeled carts from place to place. Early in the morning the *bubur ayam*

A sate *vendor gets ready for business. He will grill small kabobs of meat which are usually eaten with a spicy peanut sauce.*

man sells chicken porridge, and later the *bakso* man fills bowls with soup and bakso. These are small balls of pounded meat, chicken, or fish. In the evening the *putu* man can be seen selling a sweet of steamed rice flour, tapioca, melted brown sugar, and shredded coconut. The *sate* man grills shreds of marinated and seasoned meats, skewered on small sticks.

Some foods are sold from permanent stands. One example is *martabak*, which is a flaky meat and egg pancake.

Warungs are small outdoor roadside cafes where four to six people can sit around a table. Some warungs have only drinks, but others serve soups and rice dishes as well. These are cooked in the house of the warung owner and then brought to be sold.

There are, of course, restaurants where foods are cooked to order in the kitchen. Some of these restaurants are simple and cheap, while others are expensive. A few fast-food restaurants such as Kentucky Fried Chicken are also appearing.

Indonesian cooking is very tasty, but many poor people cannot buy enough of the right foods for good health. The poorest people rely on the cheapest foods like cassava and rice for most of their nutrition. These are filling foods but lack many of the nutrients people need.

Roadside warungs, *as shown in the picture, are everywhere. They sell drinks and sometimes food. The machine with a wheel handle (small table left) is for crushing ice. Coconut leaves are woven to make mats like the one that forms a "roof" for this warung.*

6 Caring for People

People who do not eat enough healthy food are less likely to live a long life. There are also other reasons why poorer people generally have less chance for good health. Infectious diseases that are no longer a problem in richer countries still cause ill-health in poorer countries like Indonesia. There are also some diseases like malaria that are health hazards mainly in tropical countries. Malaria can be spread when a type of mosquito bites a person.

For all these reasons, someone born in Indonesia can only expect to live an average of about 54 years. This compares with the average of about 74 years that a person in the United States could expect. Only about 17 percent of Indonesian people live to age 65 or over, compared to about 80 percent for people living in the United States.

Health services

Another way of looking at the health of a country's people is to look at the babies and young children. In very poor countries of the world, many babies do not live to their first birthday. The average for poor countries as a whole is about 88 babies dying per 1,000 live births. The average for richer countries like those in North America is only about 11 babies dying per 1,000 live births. Indonesia's average is about 90, which is high but better than in many other poor countries. Although child health has been improving, many infants still die, especially in poorer areas. In Java, some village children wear

Patients wait to see a village doctor.

cotton threads called *lawe* and charms around their necks or waists. People believe that lawe protect children from illness and early death.

A volunteer movement called *Pembinaan Kesejahteraan Keluarga* (PKK) has set up some village health services for mothers with children under the age of five. Young children are weighed monthly to see if they are growing properly. Mothers are taught which foods are needed for good health, and vitamin A is distributed to help good nutrition. Children receive vaccinations to help protect them from infectious diseases, like polio and measles. Special salts are distributed to help control diarrhea, which kills many children in poor countries of the world. Family planning services help mothers have fewer children.

Although children are now healthier than they used to be, there are still problems. In a country like the United States there is about one doctor for every 410 people. In Indonesia, there is only one doctor for every 10,300 people. This is not very good even compared to most poorer countries. For example, nearby Malaysia has about one doctor for every 3,400 people.

More doctors are being trained and the government is gradually increasing general health services. There are now over 5,500 public health centers for people in rural areas. Mobile health centers travel around to help some of the many people who live too far from a permanent health center.

Herbal medicine

Shamans or traditional "witch doctors" are still used by many people on the islands. Among the Dayak people, the shamans are old women who are thought to have powers to heal the sick. The women perform ritual dances and chants, and use herbs and plants. Various spices are used to help cure illness. Cloves are mixed with coconut oil and this mixture is rubbed on the skin to keep away mosquitoes. Cloves are also applied to the skin to treat rheumatism. Turmeric is put on cuts to stop infection and cumin is used on the forehead to help cure fevers and headaches. White pomegranate is used to help people suffering from hookworms and tapeworms.

This kind of traditional herbal medicine is called *jamu*. It is used to make cosmetics as well. Jamu women sit on the streets selling their bottles of homemade, herbal health drinks. Indonesia's government has a "Live Pharmacy" program that encourages people to make use of the space around their houses to plant herbs.

More doctors and medicines form only part of what is needed to help Indonesians to become healthier. One main source of illness in Indonesia is unclean water. Many people do not have running tap water in their homes. They have to go

Young girls come to a village water faucet to fill their buckets. They learn at an early age to balance their buckets for what may well be a long walk home. The government is trying to supply more clean water.

57

to a public tap or river to collect water and bring it home. Every day, young girls and women can be seen carrying water in plastic buckets and other containers, balanced carefully on their heads as they walk home. Their water must be boiled to make it safer for drinking, cooking, and washing. Cholera and gastroenteritis are just two of the diseases that can be reduced when people have cleaner water. Hepatitis, a disease of the liver, is another illness that can spread through contaminated water.

Keeping clean

Indonesians take pride in keeping clean and most people bathe twice a day. Bathing is usually splash-style, using cool or sun-warmed water. The *tempat mandi* or bathing place may be a Western-style bathroom but it is more likely to be a small room at the back of the house, a space outside enclosed by woven mats, or just a place by a river. People take their own towel, soap, and shampoo to the bathing spot.

For indoor bathing there is usually a *bak mandi*, which is a cement or tiled container holding bath water. A *gayung* is a tin can or small plastic bucket used to scoop out water from the bak mandi. People stand in their rubber thongs and soap and splash themselves. There are showers and bathtubs with hot water in luxury hotels, but most Indonesians and tourists staying in less expensive places rely on the bak mandi.

In Bali, village people often bathe outside in streams and rivers, men separately from women. It seems very public, but people are polite and do not look at other people while they bathe.

A woman washes clothes in a stream. The water looks clean and clear but very often it is polluted. People may catch diseases from microorganisms in water like this.

Luxury hotels have Western-style toilets but most Indonesians use just a hole in the ground, with footrests on either side. Over half the world uses this kind of toilet. People use the *left* hand only to wash themselves after the toilet—which is why only the *right* hand is used for eating.

Education

Health is also improving as people learn more about what causes disease. In the early 1960s, less than half of the people of Indonesia could read and write. By the 1980s, over 85 percent of people in cities and towns and nearly 70 percent of those in rural areas could read and write. Many more people have had the chance for education in recent years. Primary school is for children aged 7–12 in Indonesia. Junior secondary school is for those aged 13–15 years. Senior secondary school is for young people aged 16–18 years. There are state universities and institutions for higher learning as well as private institutions.

Many more schools are being built but there are still not enough. In some places primary school children use a school in the morning while older secondary school pupils use the same building in the afternoon. For example, in Bali a ten-year-old child goes to primary school from 7:00 in the morning until noon. There are about 40 pupils in her class. Her parents pay a very small fee each month. When she goes to secondary school, she will start to learn English and her school hours will be from 12:30 until 5:30 in the afternoon. The parents have no car to take her to school. Like most other children, she walks.

This class of 13 year olds is at a Balinese village school. There are just plain, wooden desks and a blackboard at the front of the room.

7 Bicycles to Satellite TV

The very oldest way to travel or carry a load is by walking. Women in Indonesia still usually put loads on their heads, from a pile of firewood to a huge basket of fruit. Men use a long pole balanced over one shoulder, with half the load hung from either end. People also ride bicycles, and amazing loads are sometimes carried on these. Motorcycles are popular on Bali and Java and some other islands. These often carry a whole family—a man, woman, and two small children.

Public transportation

This three-wheeled bemo carries passengers on a set route across town.

Few families in Indonesia own a car so public transportation is used by nearly everyone. *Bemos* are small vehicles with a driver in front and two

61

rows of seats behind. The bemos drive along set routes, picking up and dropping off people and goods along the way. Travelers can stop a vehicle as it drives by, and when a passenger wants to get off, he or she just shouts. A bemo may be full of people, chickens, caged birds, baskets filled with fruit, and even bicycles—all squashed in to carry as much as possible! People pay the driver according to how far they go.

Another small vehicle used in many towns is called a *becak*. This is a three-wheeled cycle-rickshaw with the driver pedaling at the back. A *bajaj* is a three-wheeled vehicle with the driver at the front, a motor-bike engine below, and seats for two people. *Dokars* are two-wheeled horse-driven carts that are found all over the islands. They are usually brightly decorated and jingle with bells. Smaller horse-drawn carts like the *bendi* can carry only two passengers.

Somewhere beneath all the household brushes and buckets is a man on a bicycle! The seller goes from village to village.

Ketut Watininusih is wearing the helmet and Kusma Dewi is about to share a ride on her scooter. Both girls are 18 years old.

Bemos are common in cities and also on the routes between cities. Small mini-buses called *colts* are also widely used, and there are sometimes larger buses as well, mainly on Java. Trucks with rows of bench seats in the back are used for public transportation on rougher roads. There are many good, surfaced roads on islands like Java and Bali, but on outer islands and less-traveled areas of main islands many roads are still poor. They have pot-holes and trenches, and in the wet season are rivers of mud. Cars rented to tourists in Bali are usually jeeps that can handle rough roads.

Indonesian traffic drives on the left-hand side of the road—as in Britain, Australia, Japan, and most of Southeast Asia. Problems for drivers can include stray animals and children wandering onto roads, vehicles at night with no lights, and streets with no traffic signs.

The only trains in Indonesia are on the islands of Java and Sumatra. Several airlines fly passengers between the islands and Garuda is the international plane service.

Television and radio

Just as roads and transportation are improving, so are communications. Television started in Indonesia in 1962 and now reaches about 62 percent of the people. The state-owned TVRI (Televisi Republik Indonesia) broadcasts about eight hours a day. Nearly half the programs are light entertainment but there are also news and information. Over a quarter of the programs are educational and religious. There are television sets in public places as well as private houses. For example, people waiting for medicine at a pharmacy can sit and watch TV.

The state-owned Radio Republic Indonesia (RRI) began in 1945 and now reaches about 80 percent of the population. RRI carries information on farming, health, the environment, and even family planning.

Kentucky Fried Chicken has become a popular fast-food restaurant in parts of Indonesia. The satellite dish outside provides some nearby televisions with programs from North America and Europe. The woman carries an umbrella for shade from the hot, tropical sun.

Newspapers and magazines

There were few Indonesian newspapers and magazines before the 1940s, as only a small part of the population could read. When Indonesia became an independent nation, more periodicals began to appear. By the mid-1980s there were over 200, some published daily, some weekly, and some monthly. Periodicals, television, and radio all now offer some entertainment, but people still take part in more traditional amusements. Indonesians also enjoy sports and the arts.

8 Sports and Puppets

On the island of Madura, off the East Java coast, people go to watch bull races. A jockey on a wooden sled drives a pair of bulls in a contest against another jockey. This is run as a competition involving the whole island. Elimination races take place locally and start in April. The winning bulls are matched until there is a Grand Final at the island's capital.

Horse racing is popular in West Sumatra all year round. No saddles are used and jockeys wear traditional costumes. Another entertainment in West Sumatra is bullfighting, and this is the only place in Indonesia to have this sport.

Bullfighting in West Sumatra is very different from bullfighting in Spain. In Sumatra, the bulls, or sometimes water buffalo, don't get hurt. Two bulls of about the same size are let loose to chase each other around and fight with locked horns in an open field. Finally one bull gets tired and runs away, leaving the other bull as the winner. Local people bet on which bull will win and crowd in to cheer on their favorite.

Fights

Ram-butting fights are popular in West Java. Gongs and drums are banged noisily as two rams charge at each other, clashing their horns. The losing ram is the one that is knocked out. Most villages have ram-fight societies and there are organized contests every few weeks. People like to bet on which ram will win.

In some parts of Indonesia there are fights

between men, as a sport. In Sulawesi, an unarmed contest called *sisemba* involves opponents kicking each other until one gives in! Fights are held between individuals and also between teams. Sometimes hundreds of men may be in the contest at once.

Other contests include one where the opponents hit each other with wooden clubs, and another where opponents use pairs of rattan cane. People stand at the sidelines, cheering and hoping their favorite won't be hurt.

This open-fronted shop sells sports shoes, balls, and other equipment. Many shops are open in this way. A metal door rolls down to cover the shop when it is closed. Big stores in cities now have fixed prices but bargaining or asking for discounts in smaller shops is usual. Bargaining for a lower price is also common when buying from street stalls.

Other sports and amusements

A popular sport in Sulawesi is *takro*. A rattan ball is bounced over a bamboo stick about three feet high off the ground. This is like volleyball but with only two or three people playing. Only the head or legs may be used to bounce the ball.

Ordinary volleyball is played in Indonesia as well, with large teams and crowds cheering the players. Soccer, badminton, tennis, and table tennis are also popular. Kite-flying is another favorite activity, with adults as well as with children. Young people have few store-bought toys but make their own amusement in other ways. For example, a village boy may be seen proudly balancing beside the road on homemade wooden stilts. Nearby, two men sit beneath a tree playing chess.

Music

Music is enjoyed both by those who play and those who listen. An orchestra in Indonesia is usually a *gamelan* orchestra and this is quite different from a North American or European orchestra. The name "gamelan" comes from the Javanese word *gamel* which means a type of hammer. Nearly all the instruments are percussion instruments that are struck to make a sound. The orchestra usually plays as a background to dancing or drama, but it sometimes performs on its own.

The main instrument in the gamelan is a *saron*, a xylophone with bronze bars struck with a wooden mallet. The *bonang* is a double row of bronze kettles resting on a frame, played with two long sticks bound with red cord at the end.

Men concentrate as they play in a gameplan orchestra. There are usually 30 to 40 players on a variety of instruments. The base of this instrument is wood and finely carved.

A bronze *gong ageng* hangs on a wooden frame and there is at least one of these in a gamelan orchestra. There may also be a *kempul*, which is a small, hanging gong.

Drums are part of the orchestra as well, and most are beaten by hand. They are made from hollowed tree-trunk sections of the jackfruit tree, with cowhide or goat skin stretched across both ends.

A *gambang* has bars made of hard wood laid over a wooden frame. The bars are struck with two sticks made of buffalo horn, each with a small padded disc at the end. A *celempung* is a string instrument that is plucked with the thumb nails. The *suling* or flute is the only wind instrument used in a gamelan orchestra. The flute is made from bamboo and is held upright.

69

A gamelan orchestra in Bali is slightly different from that heard in Java or Sumatra. The Javanese gamelan usually gives formal performances, whereas in Bali gamelans play more freely and more often. The instruments are both owned and maintained by village music clubs.

Dance and drama

Music is closely linked to dance and drama in Indonesia. Dance is used to tell traditional stories and to act out the clash between good and evil. There are also ritual dances to mark important events in life such as births, funerals, weddings, and harvests.

One exciting dance drama is the *Barong*, which tells the story of the good beast Barong and the evil witch Rangda. A group of men armed with swords try to kill Rangda but she takes power over the men. They are finally saved by the good Barong, who is a cross between a huge, shaggy dog and a lion. Inside the Barong costume are two men, one as the front legs and the other as the rear legs. Rangda wears an elaborate costume as well, with large fang teeth and long fingernails. Long teeth and nails are thought to be linked with "evil" in Indonesia.

The *Legong* is a very different kind of dance. It is performed by young girls wearing tightly bound, gold brocade costumes and flowers in their hair. Their faces are heavily made-up. The story tells of a king who has taken a maiden captive. The maiden's brother begs the king to set her free, but the king refuses. Later, the brother kills the king in battle. All the dance movements are slow and deliberate, with graceful hand gestures.

The huge, shaggy Barong one of the colorful characters in a Barong dance-drama.

The warrior dance *Baris* is performed by a male, and shows the feelings of a warrior preparing to meet his enemy in battle. The male dance movements including lifting knees high and thrusting out arms as if they are weapons.

The *Kechak* dance tells a more complicated story. When Prince Rama's wife Sita is kidnapped by the king of Lanka, the prince sets out to rescue her. He is taken to Lanka by the king of the monkeys and his monkey army. Throughout the dance, a circle of men wearing only checked cloths around their waists make a chanting noise to sound like monkeys. These "chak-a-chak-a-chak" noises grow louder as they pretend to fight, and the men flutter their fingers in the air.

Sanghyang dances are trance dances that

71

started as a way of driving away evil spirits from a village. The Sanghyang is a good spirit that takes over an entranced dancer. In one trance dance, two young girls dance in a dreamlike way with their eyes shut. They dance in perfect harmony to background chanting by men. When the chanting stops, both dancers fall to the ground in a faint. A priest blesses them with holy water and they come out of their trance. In another dance, a boy in a trance dances around and through a fire of coconut husks. Again, a priest breaks the trance at the end of the dance.

A young girl dances the graceful Legong.

In West Sumatra the Minang people have a number of dances. One is the *tari lilin* or candle dance, in which a group of young girls somehow manage to juggle and balance china saucers with lighted candles on them. The girls also click castanets at the same time! The *pencak silat* dance is one that every young teenage Minang boy learns. There are various versions of this dance, but all are dramatic and aggressive. In one, two dancers pretend to be a tiger hunting its prey.

A dance found only among the Bataks of North Sumatra is the *Si Gale Gale* puppet dance, often performed at weddings. A human-sized puppet is carved from wood to look like a young Batak man and dressed in a red turban, shirt, and blue sarong. A red piece of cloth is put over the shoulders. A puppet-master called a *dalang* makes the puppet dance to gamelan music.

Shadow puppets
Puppets of various kinds are an important part of Indonesian culture. *Wayang kulit* is a form of theater using leather shadow puppets (wayang

Agus Partha, master shadow-puppet maker in Bali, is the son and grandson of puppeteers. He learned the craft at an early age. It takes him about four days to make one large puppet. When he was about six years old, the government paid for his family to go to Sumatra to live. This was part of a policy to move people to less-crowded islands. After a few years, his family moved back to Bali. ''Too many mosquitoes in Sumatra!'' he said.

means "shadow," and kulit means "leather"). Wayang is also now used to describe all dramatic plays.

The figures for shadow puppet plays are usually made from water buffalo leather. The outline of the puppet is cut and fine details are then carved out with a hammer and small chisels. Moveable arms are put on and the puppet is painted. Black lines are added and a stick of horn is attached to hold the puppet upright.

The dalang is the puppeteer. He sits crosslegged behind a white screen, with an oil-lamp used to cast shadows of the puppets on the screen. It is traditional for women and children to sit in front of the screen and see only the shadow figures moving. Men usually sit and watch from behind the screen, with the dalang.

Puppets are more than simply characters in a story, they are thought to have great spiritual power. Some puppets have power for good while others have power for evil. Good characters are lined up to the right of the puppeteer while the bad characters are on the left.

The dalang may operate dozens of figures in the course of a play. He also has to tell the story and direct the gamelan orchestra that plays along. A performance may last four or five hours, so the dalang has quite a busy job!

Other puppet plays

Indonesia is known for shadow puppets, but other kinds of puppets are used as well. *Wayang golek* uses three-dimensional wooden puppets with moveable heads and arms, and there is no shadow screen. This type of puppet is most popular among the Sundanese people in West Java. The stories told are similar to those used with shadow puppets: tales of legendary kings and religious stories.

In East Java the *wayang klitik* uses flat, carved, wooden puppets and no shadow screen. The stories tell of a handsome prince and how he became ruler.

Sometimes real people dance the part of characters, imitating the movements and speech of puppets. This is called *wayang orang*. *Wayang topeng* also uses real people, but they wear masks.

Wayang theater has been used for centuries to teach traditional stories and good behavior. Wayang is also used to teach about modern problems. Puppets may even be seen on television, talking about birth control and better farming!

Shadow puppets are colorfully painted, with gold gilding. Characters may be beautiful or comically ugly.

9 Crafts and Other Exports

The carved and brightly colored puppets used for shadow plays have been made from animal hides for centuries. This is just one of many crafts in Indonesia. The best hide to use for puppets is from young water buffalo, as that kind of hide holds the colors best. Some goatskin is used as well. The hide is stretched on a bamboo frame, dried in the sun, then scraped and smoked to remove any remaining fat. After this, the pattern is put on the hide and the leather painted and gilded. Other items, such as lampshades, are made from leather in the same way. There are centers in Java and Bali especially known for leatherwork of various kinds. Bandung in West Java is noted for making shoes. Yogya in Java is famous for embossed leather.

Other kinds of leather besides water buffalo hide, goatskin, and cowhide are used. Snake, lizard, and crocodile skins are made into handbags, cases, shoes, and belts. There are even a few crocodile farms, one in Java and one in Sumatra, where the reptiles are bred for their skins.

Pottery and marble

Pottery has been made for centuries as well. Many Indonesians still use the old method of building up the sides of pots by using coils of clay, although simple wheels are sometimes used. In the villages, pots are still dried by being left in the sun or put into a fire. One village called Kasongan in Java is famous for its wild, terracotta clay figures of elephants, snakes, strange horses, and birds.

Newer techniques are being used by some modern potteries making high-quality ceramicware. A Ceramic Research Center was started in 1950 to develop the roofing tile, ceramic, and brick industries. The Center experiments and advises craftspeople on improved methods. Marble from Tulungagung in East Java has become popular for items like vases and tables, and also for floors.

Stone-carvers in Bali make wonderfully fierce demons with long fangs. These are put by the roads and at gateways to chase away evil spirits.

Sculpture

Stone carving is yet another very old craft in Indonesia, used to decorate temples and to make statues of gods and demons. Borobudur in Java has one of Indonesia's most famous attractions. The huge Buddhist monument there was built on a hill in the eighth century A.D. and includes over 500 carved stone Buddhas.

The village of Batubulan in Bali is well known today for its stone sculpture. The villagers carve fierce demon figures with bulging eyes to put outside gates and along roads as protection from evil spirits. Carvers also make statues of national heroes and freedom fighters.

Woodcarvings can also have special meanings as well as being decorative. Carved panels are sometimes put on the outside walls of houses to keep away evil spirits and diseases and bring good fortune to the family.

As with other crafts, some places are especially well known for their woodcarving skills. The town of Jepara on the north coast of Central Java is one of these, producing boxes, furniture, and other objects. Another center for woodcarving is

Madura Island. Mas is a village in Bali where many master woodcarvers live. Each different area of Indonesia has special designs of its own for carvings.

Painting

In the past, paintings in Indonesia were mainly scroll or rectangular paintings to put in temples. The pictures all told stories from myths and Hindu tales. Colors were limited to red, blue, brown, yellow, and light ochre as well as white and black. Patterns covered every part of the picture, with scenes from the story all together.

Then in the 1930s, two European artists named Walter Spies and Rudolf Bonnet came to Bali to

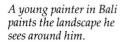

A young painter in Bali paints the landscape he sees around him.

live. Spies and Bonnet sparked a revolution in painting style. Balinese artists experimented by showing just one scene in a single picture, instead of trying to tell a whole story. Scenes of daily life became the new subjects. New ideas about painting centered in the village of Ubud in Bali, and in the 1950s a Young Artists' School came into being. Boys in their teens began to paint simple pictures with bright colors. Ubud is still a main center for painters in Bali.

Metalwork
Crafts using various metals are old as well. Bronze and iron were made into utensils and weapons centuries ago. In recent years, beautiful, useful and decorative items have been made.

Some parts of Indonesia are especially famous for their fine metalwork. People in Juwana, Central Java, make very attractive brass hanging lamps, vases, candlesticks, and bowls. Kota Gede near Yogyakarta in Java is a center for silverworking. There the silver is hammered, filed, and polished into tea and coffee sets, bowls, plates, trays, vases, and candlesticks. Yogya silverware is known for its embossed designs. A lump of hard wax is used to support the silver while the silversmith punches a decorative pattern into the metal.

Fine jewelry is made in Ujungpandang in South Sulawesi, where the rings, bracelets, and ornaments have delicate silver filigree work. Another place where filigree silver and gold jewelry is made is in Banda Aceh in North Sumatra. In Bali, a main center is the village of Celuk. Nearly every family is busy making finely decorated jewelry, often with semiprecious stones. Even children as young as eight or nine are already learning the craft. There are jewelry showrooms and workrooms everywhere in the village.

Another craft in Indonesia is making *kris* or decorated daggers, which are still part of male formal dress for ceremonies and festivals. The kris is not an ordinary kind of knife. It is supposed to have special powers and even the number of curves in the blade has a meaning. When a boy becomes a man his father gives him a kris. This is usually one that has been passed on for generations.

Ivory, bone, and horn

Jewelry and other objects are also made from ivory, bone, or horn. Part of the decoration on a kris may be carved ivory. Some people in Indonesia use ivory when a bride is given away to be married. For example, a Sundanese bride should have ivory bracelets in her dowry. The Bugis people in South Sulawesi are noted for their bone figures. Horn from the water buffalo is another material used for carvings. Several places in Bali specialize in making decorated items from both horn and bone.

Ivory comes from elephant tusks, but the number of elephants in the world has been decreasing rapidly. There is now an international effort to protect the animals. Many countries now refuse to import items made from ivory. For this reason, horn and bone are being used more and more by artisans to produce newer items and jewelry.

Items made of tortoise shell are also banned by some countries, to help protect the turtle population. In 1978 Indonesia signed an International Convention controlling trade in endangered species. Signs at airports now point out that sea turtles are becoming rare and are therefore being protected. Visitors are asked not to buy souvenirs made of turtle shell. However, tortoise shell jewelry, fans, boxes, spoons, and combs are still available in Indonesia.

Other kinds of shells are also made into jewelry and ornaments. Necklaces of *pukkah* shells are a speciality of Bali. These small, round, white shells dotted with brown are found only on Bali and nowhere else in the country. Various shells are sometimes put together on wood to make pictures. One place that is known for shell crafts is Ambon in the Malukus.

Plaiting

Plaiting, or braiding, is one of the very oldest crafts in Indonesia. Early people realized that fibers of plants could be wrapped, tied, and plaited to make baskets and other items.

Bamboo grows in much of Indonesia and is used to make furniture, musical instruments, kitchen utensils, and other objects. Older bamboo is even used for the walls and floors of village homes. It is young bamboo that is used for plaiting into hats and fans, especially in Java, Madura, Bali, and Lombok. The young bamboo is soaked in water, dried, and then split into thin layers.

Rattan is another plant fiber used for plaiting, especially in Kalimantan, Sulawesi, and

Sumatra. The fibers are soaked, dried, and split into smaller strips. Much of the rattan furniture made in Indonesia is exported.

In Bali, dried leaves of the lontar palm tree are used to make fans, hats, and bags. Dried *pandanus* leaves are used in Java and Sumatra. *Mendong* is a kind of dried straw used to make hats and floor mats in West Java. Coconut palm leaves and fibers from the coconut husk are used to make temple offerings and brushes and mats.

Textiles

One of the great crafts of Indonesia is the production of textiles. These range from the colorful barkcloths of Borneo, Irian, and Sulawesi to the silks of Sumatra, the batiks of Java, and the *ikat* weavings of the eastern islands. Each ethnic group has its own traditions.

In the fourteenth century, traders took spices like cloves, nutmeg, peppers, and woods from Indonesia to exchange for cotton and silk cloth from India. Plain, cotton weave cloth from India became common in Indonesia.

Many people in Indonesia today still wear a traditional sarong cloth in simple stripes or checks. This is wrapped tightly around the body like a long skirt. Plain weave cloth of this kind is made mostly on the north coast of Java, the north and east coasts of Sumatra, and in the south of Sulawesi.

Certain colors and designs of cloth used to be worn only by kings and nobles. There are other textiles that have always been thought to have power and magic. These are still used for ceremonies and to protect the wearer. The best known are the "ship cloths" of South Sumatra, used in wedding ceremonies and other important events. "Ship cloths" show a ship with humans and animals aboard, reflecting the traditional belief that the spirits of dead people have to go by ship to reach the land of the souls.

The most sacred textile in Bali is called *geringsing wayang kebo*, which has groups of figures and a four-pointed star. The cloth is used in ceremonies to protect the wearer from evil and illness. The word geringsing means "without sickness."

The inner bark of some trees has been used to make cloth as well. People in central Sulawesi used to boil the inner bark of pandanus, mulberry, and other trees, then beat the pulp into

Ikat weaving sometimes uses dull colors but may be brightly colored as well.

soft sheets. The cloth sheets were then dyed or painted and made into headwraps, ponchos, and bags. They still make items from plaited grass, bamboo, palm, and other leaves and fibers.

Yet another kind of textile is ikat which means "to tie." Threads are tie-dyed before they are woven into cloth. "Warp" threads are those that are stretched out on the loom. "Weft" threads are those that are woven in under and over the warp. Either the warp threads or the weft threads or both may be dyed. Ikat of the weft is usually called *songket* weaving, with a pattern in metallic, cotton, or silk thread contrasting with the background. *Songkets* are usually in bright colors and look very much like embroidery.

The best ikat weavers are the Dayak people in Kalimantan and the people of Sumba Island. There is just one village in Indonesia, Tenganan in Bali, that weaves with double ikat. Both the warp and weft threads are dyed and it is a very slow process.

Batik

The most famous textiles made in Indonesia are batiks, and Javanese batiks are the best in the world. No one knows for certain when or where this started but the Greek Ptolemy visited Indonesia in the second century A.D. and wrote about the people of Java making batik. Early batik used rice-paste to resist dye and a bamboo pen was used to put on the paste. Later, beeswax was used and then a special, mixed batik wax.

A tool called a *canting* was introduced in the seventeenth century. The canting is like a pen that holds hot, liquid wax. The wax is painted onto the cloth in fine designs. Batik that is hand-painted using a canting is called *tulis*.

After the wax is on, the cloth is dipped in dye that colors the fabric wherever there is no wax. After the first dyeing, the cloth may be painted again with wax and dyed again. In this way, the pattern or picture is built up. When all the colors have been applied, the cloth is boiled to remove any trace of wax. Women usually draw and apply the wax and men dip the cloth into dyes.

A method of making batik using a "batik cap" was invented in 1815, making it possible to produce batik more cheaply. The cap is a stamp made of copper containing the wax pattern. Batik made this way is called "batik cap" or "stamped batik." It is much quicker than hand-drawn batik tulis. There is now also machine-printed batik.

Around the year 1900, batik-making was at its busiest. At that time, almost everyone in Java wore batik. Men in government offices wore Western-style suits to work but at home they wore cotton, wrap batik sarongs.

In the past, some batik patterns were made only for rich people and nobles. There are now thousands of patterns and over 80 traditional designs. Many of these are still symbolic. For example, a batik with the pattern *sidomukti* would be worn by a bride and bridegroom at a wedding. This design is a symbol for a happy life.

The batik industry has declined slightly since World War II. One reason for this is that printed cloth, which is faster and cheaper to produce, has competed. Another reason is that some young Indonesians prefer to wear Western-style clothes. However, there is still a demand for the very fine

Lengths of fine batik cloth are sold in a Jakarta store.

handmade cloth, and batik clothes from Indonesia have been fashionable in other countries, too.

Indonesian artists began a new technique in 1966 which combines painting and the wax-and-dye process of batik. Both brushes and the canting are used to make "free-style" batik or batik painting.

Natural resources

Textiles are an important export, but the country has two other products that are bigger earners of export money. These resources are petroleum and natural gas.

Since 1980, Indonesia has been the world's leading exporter of liquefied natural gas. Three-quarters of the republic's oil production comes from oilfields on Sumatra's east coast. Sumatra also produces petroleum products and even plastics made from oil. The Dutch knew there was oil on Sumatra by the 1860s, and oil was being drilled commercially by the 1880s. A company called Royal Dutch Shell was formed in 1902. Another company, Pertamina, was started in 1957 to develop north Sumatra oilfields. By 1967 Pertamina had taken control of all the country's oil production. It is a government-run company. Petroleum and natural gas help earnings from exports and help with energy supplies for Indonesia as well.

After oil and gas, forest products are the third-largest export earner for Indonesia. The country is one of the largest plywood exporters in the world. Nearly 60 percent of the total land area of Indonesia is covered in forest. Kalimantan, Irian

This stylish furniture uses local cane and Indonesian fabrics. Products like this are being exported as well as produced for use in Indonesia.

Jaya, Sumatra, and Sulawesi are the islands with the most trees.

With so many forests, it is not surprising that Indonesia is making paper as well. In 1985, 14 new paper mills were completed, and there are now only a few kinds of paper that the country cannot produce.

Tin is another major resource for Indonesia. Since 1981 the country has been the second-largest tin producer in the world after Malaysia. Nickel, bauxite, and copper are other minerals that are mined and exported.

Besides petroleum, natural gas, timber, minerals, textiles, and other crafts, Indonesia has many other exports. The most important of these are coffee, rubber, shrimp, pepper, palm oil, tea, tobacco, electrical equipment, and cement. In 1971 a National Agency for Export Development (NAFED) was set up to promote non-oil exports from Indonesia.

Industries
A wide range of industries are developing to make goods for local people and also to make goods that can be exported. Some of the industries that showed the biggest increase in production in the 1980s were cooking oil, matches, bicycle tires, radios and cassette recorders, black-and-white televisions, refrigerators, insect sprays, fans, glasses, and bottles.

Metal industries are producing goods such as steel pipes, aluminum sheets, and machine tools for factories. Industries making transportation vehicles have been growing fast as well. Chemical industries are making such products as fertilizers and pesticides.

Trade Unions
The total labor force in Indonesia is estimated at 64 million. About 40 percent of the labor force belongs to a trade union that must operate under the control of the All Indonesia Labour Federation (FBSI). The labor force cannot go on strike as it is forbidden by law.

As Indonesia's exports grow, the country is working with other nations to improve trade. The Republic is a founder member of ASEAN, the Association of Southeast Asian Nations. This was

91

founded in 1967 with Indonesia, Malaysia, the Philippines, Singapore, and Thailand as members. Brunei became the sixth member in 1984.

ASEAN was formed by these nations so that they could help each other to grow economically and socially. Another aim is to promote peace in that part of the world. The nations cooperate in trade and also work to bring in more tourists.

Foreign tourists in Indonesia totaled over 800,000 a year in the late 1980s. Most visitors were from the United States, Australia, Japan, the Netherlands, Germany, France, the United

A rice terrace in Bali. Terracing is a way of growing crops on steep slopes. The terraces also add to the great beauty and charm of the island for visitors.

Kingdom, and Singapore. Tourism is growing and is welcomed because of the money it brings into the country. Bali and Java are the two most popular places with visitors, but other islands are attracting increasing attention. The hope is that tourists in huge numbers will not spoil what they have come to see.

Index